CW01150205

Original title:
Eclipsed Echoes

Copyright © 2024 Creative Arts Management OÜ
All rights reserved.

Author: Charles Whitfield
ISBN HARDBACK: 978-9916-90-630-9
ISBN PAPERBACK: 978-9916-90-631-6

Shards of Memory in the Twilight

In the fading light, whispers call,
Fragments of dreams begin to fall.
Shadows dance in twilight's glow,
 Carrying tales from long ago.

Echoes linger, soft and sweet,
A tapestry of time's heartbeat.
Moments tangled, woven tight,
 In the quiet of the night.

Voices Lost in the Labyrinth of Light

In corridors of shimmering hue,
Quiet wishes fade from view.
Wandering souls seek their way,
In a maze where dreams decay.

Reflections flicker, shadows blend,
Each turn a chance to comprehend.
Yet voices call from every side,
Truths entwined where hopes abide.

Serenity's Embrace in the Cosmic Gloom

Beneath the stars, silence reigns,
Whispers float through cosmic plains.
In the depths, a peace is found,
Cradled softly, a soothing sound.

Galaxies spin in gentle grace,
Time unravels in this space.
Wrapped in night's celestial glow,
Serenity's embrace starts to flow.

Ethereal Silence of Cosmic Threads

Starlit patterns weave and bend,
In their beauty, moments blend.
A tapestry of dreams held tight,
In the stillness of the night.

Threads invisible bind our fate,
In the hush, we contemplate.
The cosmos breathes a timeless sigh,
Underneath the velvet sky.

Dimming of Celestial Chords

In twilight's grasp, the stars grow dim,
Their whispers fade, a muffled hymn.
The night unfolds, a velvet shroud,
Echoes linger, soft yet proud.

The moon's ascent, a silver sigh,
Casting dreams upon the sky.
Each note of dusk, a fleeting tune,
Harmonies of the waning moon.

Hidden Harmonies

Within the forest, sounds entwine,
Gentle rustles, a secret sign.
Leaves in chorus, branches sway,
Nature's song at close of day.

In shadows deep, the heart can feel,
A melody that seems unreal.
Cascading whispers, soft and clear,
Hidden harmonies draw near.

Secrets Beneath the Veil

Behind the curtain of the night,
Mysteries dance, out of sight.
Veils of silence, softly fall,
Hushed confessions, a lover's call.

In dream's embrace, we seek the truth,
In whispered tales, the timeless youth.
Secrets buried, yet so profound,
Echo gently, all around.

Luminescent Shadows

In twilight's glow, the shadows play,
Casting light in a curious way.
They leap and twirl, a spectral show,
Painting hearts with their gentle flow.

Beneath the night, the secrets weave,
A tapestry we dare believe.
Luminescent, they softly glide,
In dreams where shadows do abide.

Ghosts of Dusk's Embrace

Whispers crawl on twilight's breath,
Shadows dance, holding death.
Faces fade in the dusky light,
Memory's grasp, a fleeting sight.

Echoes linger where dreams decay,
Lingering thoughts, they gently sway.
Phantoms move through the silver veil,
Seeking solace, how they wail.

Fading Light

The sun dips low, a final blaze,
Colors blend in twilight's haze.
Stars awake with a gentle sigh,
Embers fade as night draws nigh.

Silent whispers fill the air,
Hints of longing everywhere.
As darkness wraps the world so tight,
Hope lingers still in fading light.

Lingering Sound

In the stillness, echoes rise,
Notes of sorrow, ancient cries.
Footsteps fade on cobbled stone,
In the dark, we feel alone.

A lullaby of ghosts gone by,
Softly sung beneath the sky.
Every sigh a memory found,
Life's embrace in lingering sound.

Specters of Starlit Dreams

Beneath the night, in silence deep,
Dreams awaken, secrets keep.
Stars shimmer like distant eyes,
Guiding lost souls from the skies.

Whispers drift in the cosmic void,
Chasing hopes that time has toyed.
Specters dance in the moon's glow,
Carving paths where stardust flows.

Chasing the Dimming Sparks

Fires flicker in night's embrace,
Chasing dreams, a fleeting chase.
In the dark, shadows tease,
Fading sparks upon the breeze.

A journey through the vast unknown,
Searching for a light once shown.
Each heartbeat, a longing spark,
Yearning for warmth against the dark.

The Silence Between Stars

In the hush where shadows blend,
Whispers carry, night won't end.
Galaxies pause in the vast unknown,
Hearts beat softly, alone, alone.

Starlight dances, a fleeting grace,
Time stands still in this endless space.
Moments linger like a gentle sigh,
Breaking the silence that fills the sky.

In the dark, dreams start to weave,
Stories hiding in what we believe.
A universe held in quiet sway,
Echoes of night softly play.

Between the stars, secrets lie,
Carried on winds that never die.
In silence found, we find our way,
Guided by light till break of day.

Reflections of a Dimmed Dream

Once bright visions fade to grey,
Lost in the shadows, they drift away.
A flicker remains, a haunting trace,
In the depths of a forgotten place.

Whispers of hope, now barely heard,
On the edge of silence, a fragile word.
Memories linger, like dust in the air,
Carried by currents of deep despair.

Yet in the stillness, a spark might glow,
Awakening dreams, hidden below.
The heart clutches at what might be,
Rekindling visions of what we see.

Though shadows loom and doubts confine,
The whisper of dreams still yearns to shine.
In the twilight, a promise gleams,
Holding the remnants of dimmed dreams.

Veil of Forgotten Voices

Among the echoes, lost words roam,
Carried on winds, far from home.
Faint melodies sing of what has been,
Beneath the veil, where the unseen.

Stories murmured, secrets shared,
In corners of time where few have cared.
Each voice a thread in the fabric of night,
Weaving the darkness with gentle light.

Yet silence thickens, like a shroud,
Swallowing whispers that once felt proud.
The past drifts softly, a ghostly dance,
Lost in the shadows, a fleeting chance.

But in the stillness, a call remains,
To uncover the heart beneath the chains.
Voices forgotten, yet still they strive,
Awakening dreams that dare to survive.

Lurking in the Twilight

In the twilight, shadows creep,
Secrets lurking, hidden deep.
Silhouettes tremble, just out of sight,
Whispers echo in the fading light.

Figures dance on the edge of night,
Figures of sorrow, figures of flight.
Caught in a moment, forever they stay,
Fearing the dawn and the light of day.

The sky blushes with a distant glow,
Unraveling wonders we long to know.
In the dusk, reality bends,
Where dreams entwine and the darkness blends.

Lurking silently, they call our name,
Echoes of longing, igniting the flame.
In the twilight, we find our place,
Embracing the shadows with open grace.

Whispers in the Obscured Light

In shadows deep where secrets hide,
A flicker glows, a silent guide.
With every breath, the night conceals,
The dreams that linger, the heart reveals.

Echoes of laughter softly play,
As memories linger, gently sway.
In twilight blooms the quiet sigh,
Where hopes take flight, where wishes lie.

Within the calm, a whisper flows,
Through tangled thoughts, where stillness grows.
A dance of thoughts beneath the veil,
In muted tones, the spirits sail.

Beneath the stars, a promise swears,
In hushed tones, the universe cares.
If you listen close, you'll find your way,
In obscured light, the heart will stay.

The Last Gleam of Day

As sunset bleeds into the night,
The world is bathed in amber light.
A fleeting glimpse of fire's grace,
In evening's arms, a warm embrace.

The shadows stretch, the colors blend,
As day departs, the sky transcends.
Each moment sharp, yet soft it seems,
The last embrace of golden dreams.

Whispers of dusk in softest hues,
Entwine the heart with tranquil views.
A final bow, the sun's refrain,
The echo lingers, sweet and plain.

Yet in the dark, hope finds a spark,
A promise shines bright, a guiding arc.
The last gleam fades, but love will stay,
In every heart, the end's a way.

Veils of Stardust Silence

Under the quilt of night's embrace,
Stardust twinkles, a gentle trace.
In silence deep, the cosmos hums,
As infinite whispers softly come.

Each star a tale, a secret told,
In veils of dreams, the night unfolds.
A tapestry of light and grace,
Where time stands still, we find our place.

Hidden realms in quiet flight,
Dancing softly in the night.
Each moment draped in cosmic rhyme,
A serenade in endless time.

So let us drift where silence reigns,
In stardust dreams where love remains.
Beneath the beauty, we'll abide,
In veils of silence, side by side.

Shrouded Moments in Time

In hours lost, where shadows dwell,
Time weaves stories that none can tell.
Each fleeting glance, a memory spun,
In whispered echoes, two become one.

Between the ticks, the heartbeats race,
In hidden corners, we find our place.
Moments wrapped in softest sighs,
Where every glance is a sweet surprise.

As clocks unwind, the magic stirs,
In timeless whispers, fate deters.
A stillness grows in shrouded ways,
Where every breath remembers days.

Hold fast the now, the moments gleaned,\nIn dreams
we've shared, our worlds convened.
Through shadows lost, our spirits climb,
In every heartbeat, shrouded time.

The Murmurs Between Worlds

In twilight's hush, a gentle sound,
Ghosts of dreams where stars are found.
Winds that carry tales untold,
Whispers of the brave and bold.

Beyond the skies where secrets dance,
Visions flicker, a fleeting glance.
Hearts entwined, a soft embrace,
Lost in time, we find our place.

Shadows of the Celestial Veil

Beneath the night, the shadows creep,
Silent secrets, a vigil keep.
Stars alight in perfect form,
Glimmers fade, yet hearts stay warm.

In starlit paths where dreams reside,
Guided by the tides of pride.
Flickering hopes in a cosmic play,
Echoes of night lead the way.

Distant Whispers of the Cosmos

Across the void, a message flows,
From ancient realms where starlight glows.
A harmony of dusk and dawn,
Timeless songs that linger on.

In the dark, the galaxies call,
Softly urging us to enthrall.
Mysteries clung in the ether's arms,
A celestial waltz, a world that charms.

Chasing the Fading Light

As daylight wanes, we seek the trace,
Fleeting moments, a tender grace.
Chasing dreams on the edge of night,
Fingers outstretched toward the light.

With every dusk, a promise made,
In shadows deep, our fears delayed.
Together we turn, in twilight's glow,
Finding paths where we dare to go.

Notes from the Space Between

In the silence, whispers wend,
Through the void, where echoes blend.
Stars converse with silver light,
In the shadows of the night.

Fingers trace the cosmic lace,
Wonders in the timeless space.
Notes of dreams, both near and far,
Written in the light of a star.

Every heartbeat, a pulse of grace,
Carved in infinity's embrace.
Thoughts like comets, freely soar,
In the silence, we explore.

From the depths, the secrets call,
In the quiet, we hear them all.
Notes from places yet unseen,
Woven in the space between.

Celestial Breaths in a Dimming World

As the sun dips low and fades,
Celestial breaths ignite cascades.
Stars awaken, softly sigh,
In the twilight, echoes fly.

Moonlit whispers, gentle grace,
Time moves slow in this embrace.
Galaxies paint the night anew,
With colors bright, a wondrous view.

Each heartbeat blends with cosmic fire,
Dreams lift high, our souls aspire.
In a world where shadows creep,
Celestial secrets we will keep.

Dimming worlds, yet hearts ablaze,
In the dark, we find our ways.
Breaths of stardust fill the air,
Revealing paths beyond compare.

Secrets of the Unseen Universe

In the depth of cosmic night,
Whispers hide beyond our sight.
Veils of time and space entwine,
Secrets linger, dark and fine.

Nebulae with stories old,
Crafted by the stars so bold.
In the silence, wisdom flows,
Hidden truths that time bestows.

Galactic rivers twist and bend,
Threads of fate that never end.
We reach forth, our hands outstretched,
Grasping dreams that fate has etched.

Unseen worlds, the heart's delight,
In the shadows, we take flight.
Each secret holds a star's embrace,
Unveiling depths of boundless space.

The Fading Symphony of Stars

In twilight's glow, the music fades,
A symphony of light cascades.
Each note, a spark in distant skies,
Echoes of a world that flies.

The cosmos plays its sweetest tune,
Softly lulling the watching moon.
Stars like dancers, twirling bright,
In the heart of the endless night.

Time, the conductor, weaves the sound,
As starlight drifts from above ground.
Fading notes of cosmic lore,
In the stillness, we crave more.

As silence blooms where stars once shone,
The symphony becomes our own.
In every heartbeat, every sigh,
The fading song will never die.

Shimmers of a Distant Echo

In twilight's glow, the whispers wane,
Faint shimmers dance across the plain.
A memory lingers, soft and light,
Framing the shadows that greet the night.

The breeze carries songs that once were grand,
Lost in the silence of time's slow hand.
Reflections shimmer in the silver tide,
Where dreams and echoes forever abide.

A heartbeat drifts on the river's flow,
Pulling us gently where we can't know.
Yet in the stillness, a promise gleams,
For every whisper holds a dream.

The Veiled Rhapsody of Silence

In the realm where quietude reigns,
Thoughts weave softly like gentle chains.
A rhapsody flows, but none can hear,
In the shadows where dreams adhere.

The heart beats slow, wrapped in its shroud,
A tapestry rich, beneath the cloud.
Words are hidden in the silent air,
Waiting for time to unravel care.

Moonlight glistens on the still estate,
Where echoes linger, softly sedate.
In this embrace, we find our peace,
As the veiled rhapsody grants release.

Mirage of Stars in Dusk's Embrace

As the day fades into twilight's hold,
Stars appear like stories untold.
A mirage whispers from afar,
Rotating dreams, a flickering star.

In the hush of night, the cosmos sings,
Carrying tales on celestial wings.
Glimmers of hope in the dark surround,
Cradled in silence, a sacred sound.

Each twinkle reflects a moment's grace,
As dusk wraps stars in a gentle embrace.
In this realm of wonder, we find our way,
Through the mirage where night meets day.

The Hidden Echo of the Celestial Sphere

From the depths of night, a whisper calls,
Echoes dance within the vast sprawl.
The celestial sphere spins tales of lore,
Unseen rhythms that forever soar.

In shadows deep, where dreams may hide,
A gentle resonance flows like the tide.
The universe breathes a silent hymn,
Painting the night with its ethereal dim.

Stars pulse softly, each a hidden song,
Reminding us where we all belong.
In the heart's chamber, a secret glows,
As we listen to what the echo knows.

Phantoms of the Lunar Dance

In shadows cast by silver beams,
Whispers twirl in moonlit dreams.
Figures glide through misty night,
Chasing stars in gentle flight.

Ethereal echoes weave their way,
Through twilight skies where phantoms play.
Each movement sways, a ghostly waltz,
An ancient tale of time that halts.

Veils of mystery softly swirl,
With every step, the shadows twirl.
In the realm where silence reigns,
Phantoms dance through nature's veins.

Awake, the spirits, lost in trance,
With every heartbeat, take their chance.
In the quiet, secrets blend,
The lunar dance will never end.

The Stillness of Hidden Realms

In quiet woods where shadows lie,
The world holds secrets, soft and shy.
Beneath the leaves, stories stir,
In whispered breaths, they start to blur.

A hidden realm where time stands still,
Nature sings with a hushed thrill.
Rustling winds through branches sigh,
Echoes call from the endless sky.

Moonlit paths lead to the deep,
Where ancient beings softly sleep.
Stillness wraps around the night,
Cradling dreams just out of sight.

In this cocoon of secret peace,
Wonders wait, and worries cease.
With every heartbeat, truths unveil,
In hidden realms, we will not fail.

Veiled Sonnets in the Night

Ink-black skies hold whispered dreams,
Veiled sonnets flow in silver streams.
Each star a note, a fleeting rhyme,
Composed in darkness, lost in time.

Ghostly shadows dance and weave,
With every breath, we must believe.
In the night, the hearts engage,
As verses turn the silent page.

Softly spoken, secrets share,
Across the void, they drift in air.
A melody from ages past,
In veiled sonnets, forever cast.

Underneath the ancient trees,
Words flutter on the soft night breeze.
In nocturnal realms, we find flight,
Lost in veiled sonnets of the night.

Untold Stories of Cosmic Silence

In the depths of starry veils,
Cosmic silence holds its tales.
Whispers of worlds that came and went,
In quietude, their lives are meant.

Galaxies spin in gentle grace,
Time's embrace leaves not a trace.
Each blink, a saga yet untold,
In the void, their mysteries unfold.

Waves of silence cradled tight,
In every star, a spark of light.
Echoes of dreams from distant lands,
Awaiting hearts and open hands.

Listen close, in stillness pause,
Within the silence, find the cause.
Untold stories weave through space,
In cosmic silence, we find grace.

Reflections on a Veiled Sky

Clouds gather close, a shroud of gray,
Whispers of light begin to sway.
Beneath the shade, shadows play,
Nature's secrets held at bay.

Cascading dreams in muted hues,
Gentle breezes, silent muse.
A tranquil heart learns to refuse,
The noise of day, the endless clues.

Ripples dance on a still lake,
Mirrored thoughts, choices we make.
In the depths, the echoes wake,
Rippling reflections, life's partake.

Stillness reigns as day meets night,
Stars peek through, a spark of light.
In the veiled sky, hope takes flight,
Embracing darkness, holding tight.

The Nocturne of Murmured Thoughts

In twilight's hush, the world in freeze,
Thoughts like whispers float on the breeze.
Dreams woven softly, with tender ease,
Embraced by shadows, nature's tease.

The stars alight, high above the fray,
Cascading wishes in a soft ballet.
A serenade for night's display,
In quiet moments, hearts will sway.

Underneath the silver moon's glow,
Reflections dance in a gentle flow.
Time stands still, as secrets grow,
In the stillness, strength to know.

Melodies rise from the night's deep well,
Each note a story, too soft to tell.
In the silence, where thoughts compel,
Murmured dreams in a fleeting spell.

Echoes in the Gloaming

In the gloaming, shadows blend,
Time whispers soft, the day will end.
Colors fade as horizons mend,
In silence deep, our hearts descend.

The last light lingers, golden hue,
Leaves rustle gently, a soft adieu.
Nature pauses, as if anew,
In twilight's cloak, all feels true.

Faint echoes of laughter in the air,
Memories linger, like a prayer.
In the dusk, a gentle dare,
To hold each moment, rare and fair.

As darkness settles, a quiet throng,
Stars awaken in a soothing song.
In the gloaming, where dreams belong,
We find our peace, where we are strong.

Phantom Melodies at Sundown

When dusk descends, soft and sweet,
Whispers of twilight, a rhythmic beat.
Ghostly notes in the air repeat,
As day retreats on tender feet.

The horizon blushes, a fleeting kiss,
Melodies dance in a twilight mist.
In the fading light, a stolen bliss,
Every heartbeat is a chance not to miss.

Fading echoes of the sun's last sigh,
Nature hums a lullaby.
In the embrace of night, we rely,
On phantom melodies that softly fly.

As darkness weaves its silky thread,
In dreams awakened, spirits fed.
Sundown's grace, where hopes are bred,
In phantom tunes, our souls are led.

Faint Tones of Forgotten Realities

In shadowed corners, whispers fade,
Memories linger, colors shade.
Lost in time, the echoes crawl,
Silent stories, unseen thrall.

Between the cracks of years gone by,
Faint glimmers dance, then softly die.
Shadows weave a delicate tale,
Forgotten truths that still prevail.

The canvas worn, yet still alive,
Painted dreams, where visions strive.
A tapestry of muted light,
Stitched with threads of endless night.

In quiet realms where spirits tread,
Old echoes wake, though much is dead.
The faintest tones call forth the past,
In hidden places, shadows cast.

The Hidden Echoes of Dusk's Caress

As daylight wanes, a hush descends,
The air is thick, where silence bends.
Golden hues in twilight mix,
Nature's charm, a gentle fix.

Whispers of night begin to rise,
A serenade beneath dark skies.
Stars awaken, secrets shared,
In dusk's embrace, souls are bared.

Shadows stretch, a fleeting dream,
Moonlight spills, a silver stream.
Hope ignites in evening's hold,
With every pulse, stories told.

Through the folds of time, they weave,
In tender notes, we dare believe.
The echoes linger, soft and rare,
In the heart of dusk's warm care.

Recursive Waves in Eternal Twilight

From depths unknown, the currents swell,
Infinite tales, a silent spell.
Each wave that breaks, a fleeting shore,
In endless dance, forevermore.

Reflections caught in twilight's gaze,
The sky ablaze with fading praise.
Cyclic rhythms, a heartbeat's song,
As oceans pull, we drift along.

In mirrored realms where shadows play,
Time bends gently, lost in sway.
Recurring whispers, forever chase,
In twilight's grip, we find our place.

Tides of thought wash over shore,
Recursions weave, the mind's encore.
In waves we trust, eternal flight,
Through endless twilight, pure delight.

Beneath the Surface of Celestial Harmony

In realms where stars align and spin,
Beneath the light, the worlds begin.
Harmony sings in silent tones,
A universe that calls us home.

Within the depths of cosmic streams,
The fabric flows with whispered dreams.
Galaxies dance, a waltz of grace,
In stardust paths, we find our place.

Echoes of past, a gentle thread,
Binding lives that time has fed.
Through nebulae, our spirits rise,
In unity beneath the skies.

Synthesis of heart and mind,
A cosmic bond, so rare, entwined.
In gentle waves of light we soar,
Beneath the surface, forevermore.

Melodies of the Hidden Sky

Whispers weave through twilight's breath,
Stars awaken from their rest.
Moonlight dances on the breeze,
Carrying dreams across the seas.

In shadows deep, soft visions rise,
Glimmers hidden in the skies.
Symphonies of night take flight,
Painting echoes with their light.

Every rustle, a tale untold,
Of ancient nights and dreams of gold.
Harmonies drift through the dark,
Igniting souls with a spark.

Lost in the marvel of the night,
Where every star feels so right.
Melodies linger, softly sigh,
Awakening hopes in the hidden sky.

Murmurs of a Dimmed Horizon

Over fields where shadows play,
Whispers of dreams drift away.
A horizon dimmed, yet bold,
Holds the secrets yet untold.

Clouds embrace the setting sun,
Colors fade, but hearts stay young.
Murmurs stir in fading light,
Softly calling through the night.

Flickers of hope in distant lands,
Held within unseen hands.
Voices echo, rich and deep,
Urging souls not to sleep.

In the twilight's gentle breath,
Life and love dance close to death.
Murmurs speak of what's to come,
In the quiet, we are one.

Colliding Glimmers in the Dark

In the silence, shadows play,
Glimmers chase the night away.
Stars collide in cosmic dance,
A fragile, fleeting chance.

Jewel tones against the black,
Light and dark in wondrous track.
Every flicker, every spark,
Illuminates our journey's arc.

Hidden hopes take flight anew,
Amidst the vastness, me and you.
Echoes of our laughter roam,
As colliding glimmers find their home.

In the dark, we come alive,
Holding tight to dreams we strive.
With each heartbeat, brightly marked,
We shine as colliding glimmers in the dark.

Threads of Silence Spun in Night

Woven whispers, soft and light,
Threads of silence spun in night.
Moonlit paths gently unfold,
Carrying tales that shimmer bold.

Each heartbeat a woven seam,
Echoing a timeless dream.
Stars collide with gentle grace,
In the fabric of this place.

Hushed confessions fill the air,
In the stillness, love laid bare.
Threads entwined, a tapestry,
Stitched together, you and me.

Through the night, we tread the line,
With every thread, our souls entwine.
In silence, we find our flight,
As threads of silence spun in night.

Shadows of Forgotten Whispers

In the garden where the shadows play,
Lost voices dance, their stories sway.
A breeze carries secrets, soft and light,
Echoes of dreams in the quiet night.

Beneath the stars that fade away,
Whispers linger, they long to stay.
Forgotten tales that time won't mend,
In hushed tones, the past transcends.

Moonlight drapes the world so still,
Cloaked in silence, a gentle thrill.
As memories awaken, they softly call,
In shadows of night, we find them all.

Through the veils of dusk they glide,
Carried on wings where few thoughts hide.
Each whisper a thread, a bond we share,
A tapestry woven with tender care.

Moonlit Reveries

In the still of night, the moon's embrace,
Dreams awaken, a sacred space.
Stars twinkle softly, a guiding light,
Illuminating hearts in gentle flight.

Rippling waters reflect the glow,
Whispers of love, a soft flow.
Under the heavens, we lose track of time,
In moonlit reveries, we find our rhyme.

The cool breeze carries a sweet refrain,
Lingering echoes of joy and pain.
Each moment cherished, a treasure to hold,
In night's warm arms, a story unfolds.

As shadows dance, we twirl and sway,
In this dreamscape, we drift away.
With every heartbeat, the magic grows,
In the light of the moon, our spirit glows.

Tides of Silent Memory

Waves crash softly upon the shore,
Carrying whispers of days before.
Seas of silence, deep and wide,
Memories linger, like the ebbing tide.

Footprints washed away by the sea,
Fleeting moments, wild and free.
In the stillness, echoes play,
Tides of memory, here to stay.

The horizon stretches, a canvas vast,
Painting stories of the past.
Each wave a sigh, each breeze a tear,
In silent memory, we hold it dear.

As dawn approaches, the night retreats,
A journey ends as another meets.
Yet in our heart, the tides shall flow,
In whispers of time, love will grow.

Voices in the Twilight

In twilight's glow, the world turns gold,
Soft whispers stir, stories unfold.
Beneath the branches, shadows blend,
Voices call out, as day ends.

A cricket's song, a gentle breeze,
Nature's chorus brings us to our knees.
In the golden hour, all feels right,
Embraced by the beauty of fading light.

As stars awaken in the deepening haze,
We share our secrets in a soft gaze.
In the twilight, our hearts align,
Listening closely, your voice meets mine.

So let us linger, just a while more,
In the moments where our spirits soar.
Voices in twilight, a cherished sound,
Uniting souls where love is found.

The Subtle Dance of Light and Dark

In twilight's glow, shadows creep,
Where whispers of the day softly weep.
Stars emerge, a tender sight,
A delicate kiss from day to night.

Beneath the veil, secrets twine,
Each flicker a story, a line divine.
Moonbeams play on whispered leaves,
Guiding hearts that hope and grieve.

In every corner, contrasts blend,
Light caresses, darks defend.
A ballet of hues, a sacred art,
The subtle dance of light and heart.

As dawn awakens, they gently part,
Leaving behind a silent start.
In shadows' arms, the magic flows,
And in this realm, the silence knows.

Fractured Dreams Beneath the Starlight

Upon the canvas of the night,
Fractured dreams take fragile flight.
Each twinkle holds a path to chase,
Lost in the depths of time and space.

Beneath the stars, hopes intertwine,
Echoes of wishes, a grand design.
Moments fleeting, like grains of sand,
Written in fate's gentle hand.

In slumber's grip, illusions weave,
Tales of joy and sorrow conceived.
Each heartbeat whispers softly to,
A universe painted in shades anew.

Yet in the quiet, shadows loom,
Guarding secrets in the gloom.
Fractured dreams, though torn apart,
Find solace in the starlit heart.

Shadows that Know the Melody

In the stillness where echoes sigh,
Shadows whisper, secrets fly.
Their rhythm dances with the night,
Telling tales of lost delight.

Beneath the moon's watchful gaze,
They weave through memories, a soft maze.
With every step, they hum their song,
Binding right where hearts belong.

With every light, a shadow casts,
In harmony, they blend the past.
Notes of laughter, whispers low,
In shadows' realm, the melodies flow.

Together they sway, entwined in grace,
In this twilight, they find their place.
Shadows that know the melody's call,
Echo softly, embracing all.

When the Universe Held Its Breath

In silence deep, the cosmos paused,
Stars aligned, and fate was caused.
Time suspended, hearts beat slow,
In that moment, all hope would grow.

Galaxies whispered tales untold,
In the calm, both fierce and bold.
A breath so still, the planets turned,
In stillness, the universe yearned.

Colors bloomed in radiant skies,
Across the void, unspoken ties.
When every soul felt the thread,
And in that stillness, magic spread.

Yet time resumed, as shadows grew,
Transforming dreams with every hue.
When the universe held its breath,
Life danced on the edge of death.

When Light Flickers in Fear

In shadows deep, the whispers crawl,
A heartbeat's tremor, a ghostly call.
The dimming light, a fleeting flame,
Bound in silence, we seek the same.

With every flicker, doubt takes flight,
Lost in the swirl of endless night.
Yet in the dark, a spark ignites,
Guiding souls through forgotten sights.

Courage dances where fear resides,
Breaking chains, the heart confides.
A promise lingers in the air,
When light flickers, we learn to dare.

So hold on tight, let courage steer,
For every soul deserves to cheer.
When shadows wane, and light appears,
We find our strength, dissolve our fears.

The Twilight Whispers of Time

As day gives way to night's embrace,
The twilight whispers, a gentle grace.
Moments linger in dusky light,
Painting dreams that take to flight.

The stars ignite, each tale unfolds,
In silver threads, the world behold.
A dance of shadows, a sweet refrain,
Through every heartbeat, joy and pain.

With every tick, the clock unwinds,
Weaving memories that time reminds.
In twilight's glow, we find our way,
To hold the night, to seize the day.

So let us cherish the fleeting hour,
When day and night together flower.
For in this twilight, lives entwine,
In whispered secrets, the heart aligns.

Echoes of a Cosmic Lullaby

In the vastness where silence weeps,
Stars sing softly, the universe keeps.
A lullaby drifts through the dark,
Stirring dreams with each twinkling spark.

Galaxies sway in harmonious grace,
Their whispers linger, a tender space.
Celestial tunes, a soothing embrace,
Guide weary hearts to a tranquil place.

Through the void, an echoing sigh,
A lull of hope that will never die.
Each note a promise, each pause a breath,
In cosmic rhythms, we find our depth.

So close your eyes, let the stardust flow,
In cosmic lullabies, let your spirit glow.
For in the echoes, a truth resides,
In the heart of the universe, love abides.

Phantoms Weaved in Astral Threads

In the silence of the night,
Phantoms dance, out of sight.
Whispers wrapped in silver lace,
Drifting softly, a fleeting trace.

Stars align in fractured skies,
Veils of mysteries, ancient lies.
A tapestry of dreams entwined,
Echoes of the lost, unconfined.

Free as air, yet shadowed deep,
Carried forth in shadows steep.
Into the night, their secrets cast,
Fleeting moments, shadows past.

Timeless realms where silence reigns,
Phantoms weave through cosmic lanes.
In the fabric, hearts may find,
The echoes of the other mind.

Lingering Shadows of Nightfall's Call

Upon the dusk, where whispers lie,
Lingering shadows blend and sigh.
Hushed are the secrets, softly spun,
Beneath the glow of a fading sun.

Mists of twilight, softly weep,
Veiling dreams lost to the deep.
Crimson hues in the dark embrace,
The haunting dance of time and space.

Echoes linger, calling near,
Voices soft, yet crystal clear.
In the stillness, hearts align,
Caught in the reverie, divine.

Nightfall speaks in tones so low,
Guiding souls where shadows flow.
In this realm where spirits dwell,
Lingering whispers cast a spell.

Illuminations Lost to the Void

In the depths where silence thrives,
Illuminations dim, yet alive.
Flickers of hope in endless night,
Dancing softly, fading light.

With every star that slips away,
Dreams are woven in shades of gray.
Fading echoes of what has been,
Lost in the folds of where they've seen.

The void calls with a mournful sigh,
Yet through the darkness, sparks still fly.
In that space where wishes roam,
Hearts remember they are home.

Timeless tales begin to unfold,
In the warmth of the shadows' hold.
Each memory, though it may fade,
Leaves an imprint, never betrayed.

The Sound of Stars Turning Cold

Listen close to the midnight air,
The sound of stars, a yearning flare.
Whispers fade in the cosmic chill,
Echoes of life held still.

In the void where silence dances,
Hearts once bright now lose their chances.
Time drifts soft like falling snow,
The light retreats, a fading glow.

Colors shift in the night's embrace,
Fleeting moments lose their place.
Stars once warm now distant sighs,
The sound of dreams that slowly dies.

Yet in the cold, a fire remains,
A memory that softly gains.
For even in twilight's embrace,
The sound of stars still finds its space.

Hallowed Interludes

In quiet grace, the moments bend,
A timeless dance, where spirits blend.
With whispered secrets softly spoken,
In every heart, a promise broken.

The candle flickers, shadows play,
Each thought a star that drifts away.
The echoes linger, soft and light,
As day consents to fall to night.

In twilight's hush, we breathe in deep,
While sacred memories start to seep.
Around us swirls a gentle mist,
A fleeting glance, a lover's tryst.

Here in the stillness, we find our home,
In hallowed interludes, we roam.
With every pause, a world unfolds,
In silence deep, our truth beholds.

Shadows' Lament

Upon the canvas of the night,
Shadows dance, a sorrowed sight.
In whispers soft, they share their pain,
A tale of love that falls like rain.

Once vibrant hues, now faded gray,
Memories lost, they drift away.
With every tear, the darkness grows,
In silent sighs, the heartache flows.

The moonlight weeps for what has passed,
In shadows deep, our hopes contrast.
They mourn the dreams, the joy entwined,
In the lament of what's left behind.

Yet in the gloom, a spark remains,
A flicker bright amidst the chains.
In shadows' grasp, we find our way,
To rise anew, beyond the gray.

Chords of the Dimming Day

As daylight wanes, a symphony,
Chords of dusk, a gentle plea.
The skies alight with hues unknown,
In twilight's grasp, we feel alone.

The earth exhales, the shadows creep,
In whispered notes, the memories seep.
With every breath, the silence swells,
A melody of secrets, it tells.

Under the stars, the silence sings,
Of all the love that twilight brings.
In every chord, a heart will sway,
To rhythms soft of dimming day.

As night enfolds the world in dreams,
The music flows like silver streams.
In chords of dusk, we find our way,
To serenade the end of day.

Echoes of the Hidden Sun

In whispered winds, the stories flow,
Of suns concealed, their ancient glow.
Through cracks of shadow, light will seep,
In echoes soft, the secrets keep.

The dawn will break, a golden thread,
Weaving warmth where dreams have bled.
Though hidden suns may shroud their fire,
Their warmth ignites a fierce desire.

In each heartbeat, a distant tune,
A lullaby sung beneath the moon.
With every sigh, the past will hum,
In echoes clear, the hidden sun.

So raise your gaze, let spirits soar,
For hidden suns will shine once more.
In every shadow, light will run,
To guide us forth, our battles won.

The Ghosts of Celestial Harmony

In the twilight's gentle glow,
Whispers of stars weave and flow.
Echoes of dreams, soft and bright,
Dance through the canvas of night.

Flickers of hope in shadows hide,
Where mysteries of life abide.
Each pulse a story, each breath a song,
In the cosmic rhythm, we all belong.

Faint murmurs of the past we hear,
Guiding us with warmth and cheer.
The echoes linger, timeless and vast,
As we wander, spellbound, through the vast.

Together we sing in the starlit breeze,
The ghosts of harmony, forever at ease.
In the depths of night, where silence swells,
We find our peace; the universe tells.

When Light Meets the Abyss

In the depth of the shadow's embrace,
Light flickers, a fragile trace.
Embracing the void with hesitant grace,
Hope and the dark share a silent space.

Glimmers of dawn on the edge of night,
Fight against fears and take flight.
Each moment a battle, each heartbeat a plea,
Where light confronts what we cannot see.

Echoes of thoughts in the swirling black,
Life's brilliant spark, a guiding track.
Dancing with darkness, two souls entwined,
In the canvas of chaos, all love defined.

When worlds collide, a miracle brews,
From the depths arise vibrant hues.
Together they flourish, a radiant kiss,
In the realm where light meets the abyss.

Echoes Beneath the Astral Veil

Underneath the starry dome,
Whispers of vagrant spirits roam.
Each twinkle a tale, a journey told,
In the silent vaults of the bold.

Winds of the cosmos carry their sighs,
Secrets and dreams that never die.
In the hush of the night, they weave their threads,
Creating a tapestry where no one treads.

Veils of wonder, secrets embrace,
Among the stars, we find our place.
Guided by echoes, we rise and fall,
Listening closely, we hear the call.

In the dance of the cosmos, we sway and bend,
To the rhythm of echoes that never end.
Beneath the veil, in silence we dwell,
Finding solace where spirits compel.

Luminous Shadows in a Dusk

As the sun dips low in a painted sky,
Shadows stretch forth, as if to fly.
The twilight whispers secrets sweet,
A merging of day and night, bittersweet.

Colors blend in soft embrace,
Where light and shadow find their space.
In the fading glow, dreams take flight,
Luminous shadows dancing with delight.

With each heartbeat, the world slows down,
In the dusk's embrace, no need for a crown.
Magic emerges in the cooling air,
As everything glows, with love to share.

In this gentle hour, we breathe, we feel,
The wonders of dusk, our hearts reveal.
In luminous shadows, we find our way,
Through the twilight dance, we forever sway.

Resonance of the Lost

Whispers travel through the night,
Memories drift like paper kites.
Echoes of laughter, silent and frail,
Stories linger where dreams set sail.

The stars above hold secrets vast,
Shadows wane, but never pass.
Footsteps echo on empty streets,
Time remembers what heartbeats meet.

Flickers of hope in the misty glow,
Carried by winds that gently blow.
Voices call from the depths of time,
In lost resonance, we find our rhyme.

Song of the Hushed Horizon

Beyond the edge where day meets night,
Colors blend in a fading light.
A song drifts through the silent air,
Of lost wishes and whispered prayer.

The horizon waits with bated breath,
Carving lines between life and death.
Clouds cradle dreams, soft and low,
As twilight's hand begins to show.

With every note, the night unfolds,
Tales of wonder, daring and bold.
In the hush, a melody lies,
Echoing softly in starlit skies.

A Serenade for Shadowed Souls

In the darkness where secrets creep,
Silent shadows among the deep.
A serenade for those who roam,
Finding solace far from home.

Moonlight dances on the cold stone,
Whispers hum in a gentle tone.
Fleeting shadows, lost in grace,
In the quiet, we find our place.

With every note, the night ignites,
Embracing the beauty of hidden sights.
Together we weave through paths unknown,
In this serenade, we are not alone.

Dances with the Dark

In twilight's grasp, we start to sway,
Veils of shadow guide our way.
With every turn, the darkness sighs,
A waltz of dreams beneath the skies.

The moonlight's kiss brings forth the night,
As we dance under silver light.
Our hearts entwined, we journey near,
In the dark, we confront our fear.

Letting go, we embrace the void,
In this dark, our souls are buoyed.
Together we dance, fierce and free,
In the dark, we find unity.

Songs of the Silenced Stars

Whispers of light in the vast night,
Flickering hopes lost from sight.
Beneath the blanket, silence weeps,
Echoes of dreams that the cosmos keeps.

Floating in darkness, oh, how they gleam,
A tale of togetherness, a unspoken theme.
Each twinkle carries history untold,
A melody haunting, both gentle and bold.

Once brightly shone, now hidden so far,
Prayers and wishes, our guide from afar.
To worlds unknown, their secrets they lend,
Infinite stories that never shall end.

The night enwraps them, a lover's embrace,
As we gaze upward, we long for their grace.
In every heartbeat, their shadows reside,
A universe vast, where love cannot hide.

Night's Cloak Over Shattered Dreams

The moon hangs heavy, cloaked in despair,
While echoes reverberate through the air.
Once vibrant hopes now lay scattered and worn,
As stars mourn the dreams that we once had born.

Shadows dance softly on pathways of grief,
Remnants of wishes, a flicker of belief.
Night wraps its arms around tears we have shed,
A symphony of sorrows, the words left unsaid.

In the stillness, we search for a light,
To guide us through this enveloping night.
Yet amid the darkness, fragments remain,
Scattered like dreams lost in tempestuous rain.

Breathless with longing, we cling to the past,
Fleeting reflections that fade far too fast.
But in each heartbeat, a glimmer persists,
A thread of hope woven through shadows' twists.

The Aftermath of Celestial Gradients

Colors collide in the vast cosmic swirl,
Painting the heavens as galaxies twirl.
In the aftermath, whispers of fate,
Echo through space, a journey innate.

Stars once ablaze, now flicker in time,
Remaining a part of existence's rhyme.
Celestial wonders, a canvas divine,
Show us the beauty where dreams intertwine.

The hues of twilight embrace the unknown,
Crafting new worlds from the seeds that were sown.
In the spectrum of night, there's magic to find,
Boundless horizons where hearts are aligned.

Each gradient tells of a tale yet to be,
Of lives intertwined in the grand tapestry.
Through the aftermath, we discover our place,
In the silence of starlight, we sense their grace.

Serene Shadows of A Forgotten Past

In twilight's embrace, shadows gracefully dance,
Memories linger, caught up in a trance.
The whispers of time rustle through the trees,
Carrying secrets on the cool evening breeze.

Faded echoes of laughter float through the air,
Lingering traces of joy and despair.
Each shadow reveals a story long lost,
A tapestry woven, despite the great cost.

The moon watches over with a tender gaze,
Illuminating paths through the foggy haze.
In stillness we ponder, both heavy and free,
The ghosts of our memories, a part of the sea.

With each step in silence, we walk hand in hand,
Through serene shadows, together we stand.
Though time may forget, and seasons may change,
The echoes of love still vibrate, rearranged.

The Darkened Symphony of Distant Worlds

In twilight's grip, the echoes call,
A symphony from worlds that fall.
Notes of sorrow, chords of light,
Weaving shadows through the night.

Stars aligned in silent grace,
Each whisper tells of time and space.
Galaxies hum a mournful tune,
While dreams take flight beneath the moon.

The cosmic dance of fate unfurls,
In the stillness, the mystery swirls.
A haunting song of ages past,
In memories of shadows cast.

As darkness deepens, hearts take flight,
In the darkened symphony of night.
We become a part of the sound,
In distant worlds, our souls are found.

Faded Light

In the corners where the shadows creep,
Faded light begins to weep.
Whispers of a time once bright,
Now lost beyond the reach of sight.

Old photographs in dusty frames,
Remembering laughter, calling names.
Every beam, a tale untold,
Of warmth and dreams that once were bold.

Yet in the dusk, a spark remains,
A flicker born from heart's refrains.
Illuminating paths anew,
Guiding souls with hope imbued.

Faded light, though dimmed and frail,
Still carries echoes, soft and pale.
In every shadow, a glimmer bright,
Reminding us of love's pure light.

Fragmented Memories

Pieces scattered, moments lost,
In the mosaic of time, we pay the cost.
Shattered echoes dance and play,
As whispers of what slipped away.

Each fragment holds a story dear,
A laughter shared, a hidden tear.
In the cracks of time, we find the grace,
Of fleeting joy in life's embrace.

Yet within the shards, hope still shines,
Reconstructing dreams through tangled lines.
Amidst the chaos, we piece it right,
With resilience as our guiding light.

Fragmented memories, though torn apart,
Reveal the beauty of a beating heart.
In every splinter, a lesson learned,
In the quiet night, our spirits burned.

Whispers of a Starlit Night

Beneath the stars, the secrets hum,
In gentle winds, the night is spun.
A tapestry of dreams takes flight,
In the whispers of this starlit night.

Mysteries twinkle in the deep,
As constellations softly weep.
Each shimmer tells a tale to share,
Of love and loss, of hope laid bare.

The nightingale sings a lullaby,
To the moonlit sky, as time drifts by.
With every pulse, the universe spins,
A reminder that in silence, life begins.

Whispers linger in the cool night air,
Carrying dreams, both light and rare.
In starlit realms, our hearts ignite,
Bound forever by this endless night.

A Dance Beneath the Hidden Sun

In shadows cast where light does hide,
A dance unfolds with grace and pride.
Steps echo softly on the ground,
In the rhythm of lost dreams found.

The whispering winds guide our feet,
As heartbeats sync to time's soft beat.
Each movement tells of love untold,
In the warmth of a sun, fierce and bold.

Beneath the veil of twilight's cloak,
The silent stories of life evoke.
A fiery glow, yet cooler still,
In the dance of fate, we find our will.

A dance beneath the hidden sun,
In shadows deep, our lives are spun.
Together we twirl, rise, and fall,
In the light of love, we conquer all.

The Lurking Light in Twilight's Grip

Beneath the dimming sky so wide,
The shadows dance where secrets hide.
Fleeting whispers, soft and low,
In twilight's arms, the mysteries grow.

A glow emerges, faint and shy,
Hints of dreams that flicker by.
Night's embrace, a gentle kiss,
In the dusk, we find our bliss.

The stars awaken, one by one,
As the day's last breath is done.
In the twilight's soft, warm light,
We chase the dreams that take to flight.

Through shadows cast by fading sun,
The lurking light now has begun.
With every heartbeat, time stands still,
In twilight's grip, we feel the thrill.

Dreams Lost in the Void of Space

Drifting softly in endless night,
Stars like candles, burning bright.
Yet within their distant glow,
Dreams are lost, like whispers blown.

Galaxies twist in cosmic prayer,
A silent void, a weightless air.
Echoes linger of what once was,
In this vastness, a solemn pause.

Black holes swirl with timeless grace,
Swallowing dreams in endless chase.
Fleeting thoughts like meteors fly,
In the expanse, we ask why.

From the depths of cosmic fears,
We reach for hope, drown in tears.
Yet still, we seek, in dark's embrace,
To find the dreams lost in space.

A Melody of Faint Celestial Chimes

In the stillness, soft and clear,
Celestial chimes begin to appear.
The universe whispers tales untold,
In harmonies of silver and gold.

Stars collide with gentle grace,
Creating music in the vast space.
Echoes shimmer through the night,
Each note a spark, each wave a light.

Twinkling notes play sweet and low,
A symphony in the cosmic flow.
With every breath of cosmic air,
We dance to the melody laid bare.

In our hearts, the echoes play,
A serenade, night turns to day.
And in the silence, we find our time,
A melody of faint celestial chimes.

The Secrets Swallowed by the Night

The moon hangs low, a silver veil,
Guarding whispers, soft and frail.
In the dark, secrets intertwine,
Lost in shadows, they quietly shine.

Echoes of laughter, sighs, and dreams,
Swallowed whole by night's dark seams.
Every star a keeper of lore,
Holding tight what we can't explore.

In the quiet, our hearts confess,
Held by night's enchanting dress.
Each moment a flicker, a fleeting sight,
As secrets whisper, swallowed by night.

Beneath the cloak of endless skies,
We uncover truths, we unveil lies.
And in the silence, we find our right,
To embrace the secrets swallowed by night.

Shattered Echoes of Dying Suns

In twilight's grip, the last light fades,
Galaxies whisper of ancient trades.
Stars crumble softly, like dreams in flight,
Fading embers dance, lost to the night.

Fragments drift in the cosmic sea,
Memories haunted, they call to me.
Silent prayers in the dark, we send,
To the dying suns that will never mend.

Time unwinds in a shimmering haze,
Guiding lost souls through the endless maze.
Each echo resonates, a final song,
In the quiet void where we all belong.

So let us gather the light that remains,
Embrace the shadows, accept the pains.
In shattered echoes, new hopes will rise,
From the ashes, we'll learn to realize.

In the Grip of Celestial Mutations

Twisting forms in the cosmic dance,
Life evolving in a fickle chance.
Stardust weaves through the fabric of time,
In celestial whispers, we find the rhyme.

Nebulae cradle the dreams of the bold,
Stories of futures yet to unfold.
Under the glow of a fractured sky,
New worlds awaken, while old ones die.

Gravity swells, bending the lines,
Matter and spirit in intricate designs.
Unraveling threads that once held us tight,
In the grip of change, we lose and ignite.

Chaos a canvas, forever in flux,
Art of existence; the cosmos constructs.
From mutations, beauty will surely bloom,
In the heart of darkness, we'll lift the gloom.

Whispers from Beyond the Nebula

Softly, like secrets, the starlight spills,
Carrying stories that time distills.
Echoes of voices from worlds afar,
Drawn to the beckon of a distant star.

Veils of the cosmos hide truths unknown,
In the fabric of night, our seeds are sown.
Whispers entwined with the celestial breeze,
Carrying dreams like leaves from the trees.

In the stillness, hear the call of the past,
Where ancient shadows forever last.
From the depths of ages, wisdom flows,
Guiding us gently where the starlight glows.

In the nebula's embrace, we find our fate,
With every heartbeat, we resonate.
Through cosmic wonders, love will guide,
In whispers from beyond, we'll forever stride.

Crescendo of the Invisible Night

In the silence, a symphony starts,
Invisible notes playing tender hearts.
Stars align in an unseen trance,
Celebrating shadows in a fleeting dance.

Whispers carry through the cool twilight,
Each breath a promise, a spark ignites.
The night unfolds with a velvet sigh,
To the rhythm of dreams that almost fly.

In this crescendo, emotions arise,
Painting the canvas of limitless skies.
Moments collide, creating a spark,
In the music of darkness, we leave our mark.

Let the invisible night take its flight,
Embrace the magic, the softness of night.
Together we soar, unchained and bright,
In the crescendo of love's pure delight.

Milton Keynes UK
Ingram Content Group UK Ltd.
UKHW031319271124
451618UK00007B/223